MW01170602

CONTENTS

ABOUT THE AUTHOR

Hello,

My name is Curtis Boyd, I was born and raised in Flint, MI. Growing up my whole life with ADHD, structure and routine has been one of my biggest struggle as a kid and even worst as an adult.

After all these years of being lost, feeling stuck, and not finding what truly makes me happy physically, mentally and, emotionally. I knew it was time to find a solution to this problem. I knew that I can't be the 1st or the last person who's struggling with structure and routine. So this is when my journey began and my life CHANGED in ways I didn't think were possible. Mainly over the last 5 years I have educated myself on how to be more effective in life/business/relationships on a daily basis.

This is why I have created this book to give back and share the knowledge I have gained that has changed my life, also guidance and insight on how and effective routine can supercharge your life, your mood, and the confidence needed to accomplish things you've never thought was possible.

In this book, I will help you become a master of routine. Benefits of a effective daily routine are:

- Improved time management
- Helping you to build up healthy habits
- Helping you to combat bad habits
- Stress reduction
- Improving your overall health
- Managing your financial budget

· Improving parenting skills

These are just some of the benefits a daily routine can deliver. However, you may need to tweak your routine a little in order to find what works for you. Don't expect to start a daily routine and improve your life overnight. It takes time and dedication to get used to a routine, and to find one that truly works for you.

BE PATIENT AND LET ME HELP CHANGE YOUR LIFE!

INTRODUCTION

Have you ever heard of DECISION FATIGUE?

As said by a good friend of mine <u>Tyler Bryan</u> "It basically explains why eliminating extra decision making situations, will free up your mind to make better decision in strategy planning or business".

FOR EXAMPLE:

Mark Zuckerberg wears a grey t-shirt and jeans every day. Barak Obama always wears a grey or navy suit. Tech Billionaire Elon Musk, wakes up everyday around 7am and works till 1am EVERY SINGLE DAY. <u>Daily routine not only simplifies your life but it helps with your growth as well.</u>

Why are a lot of famous and successful people so "boring"? The answer is, they've learned that creating a simple daily routine to cover the basic stuff of life leaves them free to work on the important, interesting and creative challenges that make up their life's work.

Each day, we are put in positions to make thousands of decisions - from what to eat, to what to wear, to what to buy. By streamlining some of those decisions into simple, repeatable routines, we can free up time and energy to do things that really matter to us.

Learn to make time for yourself, your routine, and GET EXCITED ABOUT LIFE!

Read on to learn more about the power of routines, and how they can help you be more productive and less stressed.

WHAT IS A ROUTINE?

A routine is any set of actions that are repeated, habitually and without much thought. Routines come in different sizes. They can be as small and simple as making your bed, or as large and complex as the daily schedule that keeps you and your family fed, cleaned, clothed, and attending your work, school, and leisure activities.

For most of us, our days are made up of various routines, stitched together overtime. We have a routine upon waking, a routine for getting to work, a routine we do when we get to the work/office, a routine at the gym, and so on.

By our very nature, routines happen on autopilot, freeing our minds for other things. After all, can you remember in detail exactly how you got to work this morning? Or did you just get there somehow, without really remembering all the steps? If you are like most people, your commute to work happens automatically. You walk to the bus or pull onto the highway while thinking about other things. It's precisely this automatic nature of routines that makes them powerful. Once we make something a regular habit, we no longer have to concentrate on it.

<u>So, the key to harnessing the power of routines is:</u>

-Recognizing those portions of each day that have become routine.

-Analyze those routines

-Are they helping you, or hurting you?

Recognize what works and what doesn't, then change your routine to improve your life in whichever way you choose - whether you want to finish your novel, get in shape, organize your life, or just have more time for your kids.

Remember that every single persons routine is different. What works for one person may not work for you. The fun part is that you can choose all the things that works BEST for YOU.

EXAMPLES OF ROUTINES THAT WORK

Many successful and creative people have mastered the power of routine to get their work done.

Early to Bed, Early to Rise, Early to Create a Bestseller

While many writers disdain the tyranny of "office jobs", some of the most successful writers in the world maintain stricter schedules than most bosses would ever hold them to. For example, Japanese writer Haruki Murakami gets up at 4 am every day and writes for five or six hours. In the afternoon, he runs, swims, or both, then reads and listens to music. He then goes to sleep every day at 9 pm. Murakami maintains this schedule for six months to a year at a time, while he is working on each book.

Even more disciplined than Murakami is American novelist Danielle Steele, who has written 179 books and counting. Steele is at her typewriter every single day by 8:30 am, nibbling on the same breakfast each day: toast and a decaf iced coffee. She keeps typing for hours, claiming to work as much as 24 hours straight when the words are flowing. Note that while this particular schedule may work well for Steele, sleep experts recommend that adults get at least seven to eight hours of sleep every night in order to be as healthy and productive as possible.

So Don't get caught up on comparing your routine to others

because every single person operates differently.

Boring Outfits, Creative Minds

While many creative professionals and entrepreneurs take wild risks in their work, in their personal lives they trust in a regular routine to relieve stress and free up mental space for more important decisions. Choosing a daily uniform is one common way that creative people limit the decisions they have to make each day.

We mentioned Facebook founder Mark Zuckerberg, who is famous for his limited wardrobe of grey t-shirt, jeans, and a hoodie. While he has been seen in a suit on rare occasions, he mostly sticks to his uniform. He claims that by always wearing the same thing, he reduces the number of decisions he has to make in a day so he can focus on more important matters.

While Mark Zuckerberg's wardrobe is particularly limited, he isn't alone in limiting his clothing choices. Designer Vera Wang, despite creating some of the most beautiful and extravagant wedding dresses in the world, limits her own wardrobe to a handful of basics, all in black. Designer Michael Kors also keeps to a sleek black wardrobe of blazer, t-shirt, pants, and loafers.

Simple Meals Save Time

Many people tend to eat the same breakfast and lunch day after day, but Norwegians take "boring" meals one step further. In Norway, almost everyone brings exactly the same type of lunch to work each day, and this habit may be one reason why Norway has one of the highest scores for quality of life in the world. Everyday around noon, almost all Norwegians reach into their packs for their matpakke(Packed Lunch), a stack of several slices of brown bread with a thin layer of butter and a slice of cheese, meat pate or smoked salmon. This stack of open-faced sandwiches is always simply wrapped in brown paper.

This basic lunch has many advantages: it can be made in a few moments; it can be carried in a backpack without harm or mess; it doesn't require refrigeration or heating; and it can be quickly eaten. This last point is key. In Norway, lunches last only 30 minutes. These short lunches help keep Norway's working hours among the shortest in the world, an average of just 38.5 hours per week, which helps boost their quality of life.

THE MANY BENEFITS
OF FOLLOWING
A ROUTINE

As the examples above show, routines can be an effective way to maximize your day. Here are some benefits of following a routine:

Avoiding Decision Fatigue

Every day, we have to make thousands of decisions. Our brains are constantly making choices, from the small (which shirt to wear) to the big (which company to award a contract to). Every time we ponder the options and make a choice, it uses a little bit of our mental energy. Our store of mental energy is finite and as it runs out, it becomes more and more difficult to make decisions. This can result in procrastination, snap decisions, and poor decision making, on top of unnecessary stress.

This is true even when we are making fun choices, such as vacation planning or picking items for a registry. For example, one study showed that volunteers enjoyed choosing fantasy items for a hypothetical wedding registry for around four minutes. By minute 12, making decisions — even fun decisions — was exhausting.

Of course, making decisions is an important part of life. After all, making decisions is how we choose our education, jobs, and life partners. So, how can we escape needless decision making and preserve energy for those choices that really matter? The answer is to set a routine you don't need to think about for the simple things, so that your decision-making abilities are saved for the important things in life.

Time Savings

Have you ever lost your keys, your wallet, or your work badge? How long did you waste looking before your items turned up?

Everyone misplaces something from time to time, but if you regularly lose important items, developing a routine can save you time. Create a place for all the daily items you need and return them to their place, every single day. Likewise, if you lose track of important documents at work, or frequently forget items on your to-do list, developing a routine for organizing and keeping track of your important papers will save you time and energy, and let you get your work done faster.

Money Savings

Do you eat lunch out every day? Or grab a daily latte and a muffin from the coffee shop for breakfast? A habit of eating out is a routine, and it's one that could be costing you a lot of money. Instead, develop a routine of buying groceries and prepping simple breakfasts and lunches once a week. You'll save time and money in the long run.

By a similar token, developing a consistent look can help you spend your clothing budget wisely, and avoid impulse shopping for clothing that doesn't suit you or your lifestyle. It can also save time getting dressed each morning. Of course, a consistent uniform doesn't have to be all boring black. Think of Angela Merkel's signature-colored jackets, Diane Von Furstenberg's brightly printed dresses, or Kanye West's color coordinated sweat suits. The idea is simply to pick something that works for you and stick to it.

Boosting Health

According to CDC, only 23% of Americans get the recommended amount of exercise each week. Adults should perform strength training exercises twice a week, as well as getting 150 minutes of brisk movement each week, equal to a 25-minute walk per day.

Even fewer Americans get enough fruit and vegetables each day, with just one in ten eating the recommended four to five cups of fruits and veggies per day. If you aren't the sort of person who wakes up feeling motivated to hit the gym and eat broccoli (and really, who is?), a routine can help.

The key to a routine is that it doesn't depend on motivation — you just do it out of habit. If you want to get healthy, make fitness and healthy eating part of your routine. For example, add a serving or two of fruit and vegetables to every meal, and when you get home from work, walk around the block a few times before you go in the door.

Helping You (and Your Child) Sleep

Another important benefit of routines is in their ability to help you get the sleep you need. If you struggle to get a full seven to eight hours of sleep each night, your pre-bed routine could be the culprit. I know it was mine for awhile. If you spend the moments before bed scrolling social media, having a drink or 2 or simple watching action films, it's no wonder it's hard for you to relax and sleep.

For the best sleep, experts recommend turning off TVs, computers, tablets, and phones at least an hour before sleep, and developing your own soothing ritual. Whether you stretch, meditate, drink warm milk(this is usually one for the kiddos), read a soothing book, or listen to a calming podcast, find something that relaxes you and do it every night. Before long, your brain will recognize your bedtime ritual, and help you drift off faster and sleep more deeply.

Getting a good night's sleep is even more important for your child. Studies show that starting in infancy, performing a bedtime ritual helps children fall asleep faster and stay asleep longer. Good bedtime rituals include a bath, brushing teeth, story time, and gentle cuddling or a massage. Studies show that such a consistent bedtime routine can help children (and their parents!) sleep better in as little as three days.

THREE WAYS THAT ROUTINES CAN HELP YOU SAVE MONEY

Can routines save you money? Well, if the routine is buying a Starbucks mocha latte every morning at the gas station, it probably won't. However, there are many ways in which establishing a solid routine can help you save money.

Here are three:

1.   A routine prevents impulse buys. For example, if you get into a routine of making your own coffee every day, it's much easier to say "no" to the pricey coffee shop on the corner. Likewise, packing a lunch is far cheaper and healthier than buying lunch out every day.

2.   Routines prevent decision fatigue that can lead to poor decisions.   Willpower isn't infinite. Studies show that we only have so much willpower to make good decisions each day and once it's gone, it's easy to make poor choices. The cure is to establish routines, so you don't have to make as many decisions each day. For example, eat the same breakfast and lunch every workday. By simplifying some choices, you save your decision-making abilities and willpower for genuinely important decisions.

3.   Routine maintenance helps prevent surprise repair bills. Whether it's your car, your home, or even your own

health, routine maintenance helps prevent big repair bills. For example, establishing a routine of good oral hygiene, including regular flossing, brushing and trips to the dentist, helps head off expensive dental work. Keeping up with cleaning and maintenance on your home, can better prepare you to foresee/prevent high repair maintenance cost. Maintaining your car, with fluid top-ups, oil changes, fresh filters, and so on, keeps it on the road for longer. Also detoxing your body and practicing proper physical and mental exercises can help prevent expensive doctor visits and damaging medications.

While routines can save you money, beware of routine expenses you don't need or want.

For example:
Do you have a pricey gym membership you don't use? A magazine subscription for something you don't read? Review all your recurring expenses. Make sure you only pay for things you enjoy and use regularly. Otherwise, if they just don't fit into your routine, cancel them.

HOW ROUTINES CAN HELP WITH DEPRESSION AND ANXIETY

Depression and anxiety are very common. Almost 7% of Americans experience depression in any given year, and around 18% of the population struggles with anxiety. Both depression and anxiety are serious — but highly treatable — illnesses.

If you are experiencing either of these conditions, it's important to talk to your doctor about treatments that can help. In addition to medical treatment, lifestyle changes can help you manage your mental health. Maintaining healthy routines is one way to help boost your mood and fight depression and anxiety.

How can something as simple as a routine improve your mental health? Here are four important ways:

1. Routines help lower stress.

When life gets chaotic, it's easy to become overwhelmed by anxiety. By maintaining a regular routine, it's easier to stay organized, lowering stress.

2. Routines help with self-care.

When you are in the grips of anxiety or depression, it can be hard to take care of yourself. Basics such as showering, putting on clean clothes, eating something healthy, cleaning your home, and going for a walk are easily forgotten. Writing down and following a simple self-care routine can help you look after yourself and will help you feel a bit better.

3. Routines help you sleep.

Poor sleep is associated with both anxiety and depression. Studies show that creating a regular pre-bedtime routine can help you fall asleep faster and get better quality sleep. The better you sleep, the better you feel. A good pre-sleep routine might include turning off TVs and other electronic devices, reading a book, meditating, stretch to reliving tension, taking a bath, and sipping chamomile tea.

4. Routines keep you active, which helps you feel better.

Physical activity is a powerful stress fighter and mood booster. In fact, for some people, exercise may be as effective as medication for mild depression (however, exercise is not an effective treatment for severe depression). For many people with depression and anxiety, establishing a regular exercise routine is the key to maintaining their mental health and wellbeing.

WE ALL struggle with depression or anxiety, rather people believe it or not. But establishing healthy routines can be one way to help yourself feel better, and do better!

TIPS FOR CREATING SUCCESSFUL ROUTINES

If you are ready to start crafting routines that work for you, here are some tips to help you get started:

Identify and Tweak Your Existing Routines

The first step is to identify the routines you already have. Track everything you do for 24hr I mean everything. This only works if we can identify ways to be more productive with our time.

Think about what you do when you wake up and go to sleep, how you make dinner, what you do when you get to the office, and so on. Are there portions of your day that are stressful, chaotic, or take far more time than they are worth? Those are the areas where you can make improvements.

For example, if you can never find your keys, make a routine of putting them in the same place every day. If making dinner takes too long because your kitchen is a disaster, start a routine of tidying up every evening before you turn on the TV. By making small tweaks like these, you'll make a big difference in your day-to-day satisfaction.

Attach Change to Existing Routines

When you want to start a new habit, one of the most effective strategies is to attach the habit to something you already do habitually. For example, if you want to start flossing and you already brush your teeth each night, floss every day before you brush your teeth. If you want to start walking for 20 minutes each day and you already take the bus, start getting off one stop early and walk the rest of the way.

Tackle Change in Small Doses

If you want to improve your health, fitness, and professional prospects, learn a new language, make all your own meals, and maybe a few other things besides, don't do them all at once.

Make a list of everything you'd like to do and decide on the one or two things that are most important to you. Start there. Now, think of one or two small tweaks to your day that will get you closer to your goal. For example, if you want to get more organized, start by tidying for 10 minutes before you eat dessert each night. Once you have successfully made one change and stuck to it for a few weeks, add another change.

Choose the Motivation That Works for You

There are many strategies for motivating a change in routine. For example:

· Make an X on the calendar for every day you complete your routine, and try to maintain your streak
· Tell a friend about your goals, and ask them to check in regularly
· Compete with a friend, to see who can stick to a plan most effectively
· Create a sense of identity around your goal; that is, see yourself as "a person who eats healthily" rather than thinking, "I have to eat another salad today, ugh…"

The key to using these strategies successfully is to recognize which ones work for your personality, and which ones don't. For example, some people love nothing more than ticking an item off a to-do list. For others, a well-laid-out to-do list makes them want to run screaming in the other direction. Some people are very motivated when someone else holds them accountable, while other people are motivated by doing things differently from other people.

When you are planning your new routine, be realistic about what motivates you, and plan your rewards accordingly.

For more information about ways to motivate habits, read Better than Before, by Gretchen Rubin, which contains 21 strategies for habit formation.

Link - https://www.amazon.com/Better-Than-Before-Mastering-Everyday-ebook/dp/B00PQJHIXM

Be Realistic about How Long It Takes to Form a Habit

The internet is full of 21- or 30-day challenges that promise to kick-start a new habit in just three or four weeks. Yet, the reality is, it can take several months for a new habit to become automatic. For example, a 2009 study of habit formation found that volunteers took anywhere from 18 to 254 days to form a new habit, with the average being around 66 days.

If you are struggling because a new routine doesn't feel like a habit yet, it helps to know that it's perfectly normal for a habit to take time to develop.

FIVE TIPS FOR SAVING TIME ON YOUR MORNING ROUTINE

A solid morning routine can help you stay organized, relieve stress, and help you get a jump on the day's work. However, if you aren't a morning person, it can be tough to establish a morning routine. Here are some time-saving tips that can help you smooth out your mornings, no matter how much of a night-owl you are.

1. Use technology. If it's tough to get going in the morning, buy programmable appliances. For example, many coffee makers can be pre-set to brew at a certain time. For breakfast, a slow cooker or an Instapot can be set the night before so you can wake up to a hot breakfast.

2. Do some morning prep the night before. If mornings are a rush, lay out your clothing, pre-pack your briefcase, and make lunch before bed.

3. Or, use weekends for prep. If weeknights are too busy, try spending a couple of hours on Sunday getting organized for the week. Look online for recipes that make enough for a week's lunches, stock up on with breakfast food, and do your laundry so your work clothes are fresh and ready to go.

4. Give your children responsibility. Even pre-school kids can gather an apple and some carrots for their lunch or pick out tomorrow's t-shirt before they go to sleep. As they get older, they

can take on other chores, such as putting oatmeal in the slow cooker for the family breakfast.

5. Aim for six or eight hours of sleep. Perhaps the best way to save time in your morning routine is to make sure you get to bed on time the night before. Virtually all adults need six to eight hours of sleep a night. If you are getting less, mornings will feel rushed and stressful because you are tired rather than because there's actually no time. After a good night's sleep, you'll find your morning routine goes much more smoothly.

HOW TO CREATE A ROUTINE FOR YOUR CHILD

Children naturally crave consistency, predictability, and structure in their days. After all, they are learning about the world for the first time, and that can be scary. Keeping their schedule consistent helps kids feel safe and secure and gives them the confidence they need to explore. To create a schedule for your child, follow these tips:

Keep It Simple

You don't need to schedule every minute. Just start by scheduling the basics: bedtime, wake-up time, nap time, mealtimes, bath time, play time, chores. Write down the schedule in big letters, add some simple pictures, and hang it where your child can see it. That way, when there's an argument about what to do next, you can simply point to the schedule.

Keep It Realistic

As you know, kids take a long time to do just about anything. Make sure that when you create a schedule, you leave enough time to get things done. If you don't leave enough time to complete tasks, the schedule will be frustrating for both you and your child.

Give Your Child Choices

Kids like to feel part of the decision-making process. So, build in opportunities for them to choose. Just make sure they are choosing between two healthy options! For example, when getting dressed, give them the choice between a red shirt and a blue shirt.

Set Rules and Enforce Consequences

Be consistent in enforcing your rules. For example, if teeth must be brushed before going to the park, you may have to skip the park if your child refuses to brush their teeth. If you are consistent, they'll soon understand the rules.

Get Everyone on the Same Page

If different caregivers follow different routines, it can be very confusing for your child. When you establish a routine, be sure to share it with anyone who takes care of your child and explain why it's important that everyone follow the plan (even you, Grandma!).

GETTING BACK ON TRACK WHEN A ROUTINE IS BROKEN

Once you've done the hard work of establishing a routine, it's just going to carry on forever, right? Unfortunately, no. No matter how well established your routine is, sometimes life happens. You may get sick, go on vacation, have visitors, or just get tired and neglect your routine for a few days. It doesn't matter why your routine was broken; the key is to get back to normal as soon as you can. Here's some tips on how:

Don't have an all-or-nothing mindset. Sometimes, if we feel we have to do something every day and then miss a day, it feels like failure. Then, negative emotions can set in, making it much more difficult to get back to your routine. However, remember that life isn't all-or-nothing. If you miss a day of your routine, it's ok! Just get back at it tomorrow.

Tweak your routine. Sometimes, we stop following a routine because it doesn't serve us well anymore. Any time you take a break from routine, think about why. If you realize that you stopped because something wasn't working, adjust as needed and try again.

Remember: sometimes a routine is a rut. While routines offer a way to get some of life's busywork out of the way on autopilot, it's important not to let everything be on autopilot. If you are so entrenched in your routine that you haven't changed your hair in a decade, or you eat the same thing for dinner every single day, maybe it's time to shake things up. Change your routine, try something new, and breathe some fresh air into your day.

A routine is any set of tasks that we perform habitually, without requiring much thought. Because it's easy to follow a routine without too much thought or stress, routines can be powerful tools for streamlining our days.

When we pick something that used to take energy - such as debating what outfit to wear or what to make for breakfast - and turn it into a routine (it's Tuesday, so I'll have oatmeal, and wear the navy suit), we free up mental energy for the important decisions in life.

By identifying areas where your life could benefit from a routine, you can harness this power of routines to help make you more productive and less stressed.

WHAT'S NEXT?

I hope you've found this guide useful. I'd recommend you print this eBook, if you haven't done so already, and work your way through each section one by one.

It's easy to feel overwhelmed at this point and feel there's a lot to think about.

Start off by deciding which part you want to start with first (it really doesn't matter … what's important is that you start) and schedule in a 60-minute slot in your diary over the next couple of days.

Create a non-distraction zone; switch off your phone, close down your email and shut off social media. Focused time will serve you well.

"You have nothing to lose."

Made in the USA
Columbia, SC
03 September 2022